SPORTS
ALL-ST★RS

JOEL EMBIID

Jon M. Fishman

Lerner Publications ◆ Minneapolis

Lerner Publications Company
An imprint of Lerner Publishing Group, Inc.
241 First Avenue North
Minneapolis, MN 55401 USA

Main body text set in Albany Std.
Typeface provided by Agfa.

Library of Congress Cataloging-in-Publication Data

Names: Fishman, Jon M., author. | Lerner Publications Company.
Title: Joel Embiid / Jon M. Fishman
Other titles: Sports all-stars (Lerner Publications Company)
Description: Minneapolis : Lerner Publications, 2020. | Series: Sports all-stars
    (Lerner Sports) | Includes bibliographical references and index. | Audience: Ages:
    7–11 years. | Audience: Grades: 4 to 6.
Identifiers: LCCN 2019028058 (print) | ISBN 9781541577299 (Library Binding) |
    ISBN 9781541589544 (Paperback) | ISBN 9781541583566 (eBook PDF)
Subjects: LCSH: Embiid, Joel, 1994-—Juvenile literature. | Basketball players—
    Biography—Juvenile literature. | Centers (Basketball)—Biography—Juvenile
    literature. | Philadelphia 76ers (Basketball team)—History—Juvenile literature. |
    National Basketball Association—History—Juvenile literature. | Basketball—
    United States—History—Juvenile literature.
Classification: LCC GV884.E52 F57 2020 (print) | LCC GV884.E52 (ebook) | DDC
    796.323092 [B]—dc23

LC record available at https://lccn.loc.gov/2019028058
LC ebook record available at https://lccn.loc.gov/2019028059

Manufactured in the United States of America
1-46751-47742-9/11/2019

CONTENTS

PLAYING WITH FIRE

Embiid races past the Raptors' Pascal Siakam.

It was May 9, 2019, and the season was on the line for Joel Embiid and the Philadelphia 76ers. They faced the Toronto Raptors in the National Basketball Association (NBA) playoffs.

FACTS
AT A GLANCE

- **Date of Birth:** March 16, 1994

- **Position: center**

- **League:** NBA

- **Professional Highlights:** chosen third overall in the 2014 NBA draft; trained with a special coach in 2018 to improve his skills; led Philadelphia to the **conference** semifinals two years in a row

- **Personal Highlights:** played soccer and volleyball more than basketball as a kid; is active and popular on social media; works with groups to help people in need in the United States and Africa

As a center, Embiid usually faces off against the biggest players on the opposing team.

The winner of the series would advance to the conference finals. Toronto had already won three games and needed just one more win to take the series. Embiid and the 76ers set out to stop them.

A center is usually one of the biggest players on a basketball team, and Embiid is no exception. He stands 7 feet (2.2 m) tall and weighs 250 pounds (113 kg). But Embiid is known more for his playing style than his incredible size. No one works harder during games. He races around the court, diving after the ball and even falling into fans on the sidelines.

The 76ers needed Embiid to play his best to beat the Raptors. He plays with a high-energy style to inspire his teammates. "This was a do-or-die situation, so I knew I had to come in with high spirits," Embiid said.

Philadelphia led for most of the game. In the third quarter, Embiid showed that he's a force at both ends of the court. When Toronto missed a shot, he soared to grab the **rebound**. The 76ers passed the ball to one another as they raced down the court. Embiid took a shot. *Swish!*

He made the basket even though a Toronto player had committed a **foul** on the shot. Embiid made a **free throw**. The play gave Philadelphia a 14-point lead.

The 76ers stayed ahead and won the game 112–101. Embiid finished with 17 points and 12 rebounds. He also blocked two Toronto shots. Amazingly, Embiid finished the game at plus-40. That meant when he was on the court, his team scored 40 more points than the Raptors did.

Three days later, Toronto beat Philadelphia with a last-second basket to advance in the playoffs. Embiid led his team in scoring for the game, but it wasn't enough. He walked off the court in tears. Embiid's passion for basketball has helped make him an NBA superstar.

CAMEROON KID

Embiid played with the Kansas Jayhawks for only one season before going pro.

NBA courts are made of wood and polished to a shine. Growing up in Cameroon, Joel Embiid played his first basketball games on a very different kind of court. The outdoor cement floor was cracked, and the hoops were bent and twisted.

Joel was born in Yaounde, Cameroon, on March 16, 1994. Cameroon is on the western coast of Africa. About 25 million people live there.

Joel enjoyed sports as a kid, but he didn't play much basketball. He preferred volleyball and soccer. Then he went through a growth spurt as a teenager, and his height caught the attention of basketball **scouts**.

Yaounde, Cameroon

Like Joel, Luc Mbah a Moute was born in Yaounde. In the 2008–2009 season, he joined the NBA's Milwaukee Bucks. Mbah a Moute started basketball camps to help support the sport in Cameroon. In 2009, Joel was 15 years old and stood nearly 6 feet 10 inches (2 m) tall. Partly because of his height, a scout invited him to Mbah a Moute's camp.

Joel was so nervous that he skipped the first day of camp. But when he arrived on day 2, he proved that he belonged. He had natural basketball skills and showed off with **slam dunks**.

Like Embiid, Mbah a Moute was discovered by scouts at a basketball camp.

Embiid cheers after making a dunk in 2013.

After the camp, Joel received a **scholarship** to attend Montverde Academy in Florida. Mbah a Moute had gone to the school, and it was a good place for Joel to sharpen his skills. But he had to leave his friends and family in Cameroon. "I was a little afraid," Joel said. "The only English I knew was 'good morning.'"

Joel arrived in the United States at the age of 16. He worked to improve his English and his basketball skills. Since he could already jump and dunk like an NBA player, he worked on dribbling, shooting, and passing. He watched YouTube videos of people shooting and tried to copy their styles.

At just 20 years old, Embiid announced he would enter the NBA draft.

By 2013, Embiid was ready for college. He joined the University of Kansas basketball team. He averaged more than 11 points and eight rebounds per game. Though his first season ended early due to a back injury, Embiid felt ready for the next level. In 2014, he entered the NBA draft.

Embiid avoids a defender in 2019.

In the past, most NBA centers were slow and didn't move around much. They used their large bodies to take up space in front of the basket.

Centers such as Embiid and Shaquille O'Neal (center) are often called big men. They are usually the tallest players on a team.

They banged, pushed, and elbowed the other team's biggest players. That all changed thanks to Embiid and other modern centers.

Embiid is tough. Like past centers, he sometimes plays near the basket and bangs into other players. But he also takes long three-point shots. He might dribble toward the basket and then pass to an open teammate. Instead of standing in one place, Embiid moves all around the floor, switching quickly between offense and defense.

Because modern centers do it all, they have to practice different skills. After the 2017–2018 season, Embiid trained with Drew Hanlen, a special skills coach. At first, they practiced the moves that centers have always been expected to know. They worked on shots and plays close to the basket.

Hanlen taught Embiid a move called the half spin. Embiid stood about 7 feet (2.1 m) from the basket, facing away. He dribbled twice and spun quickly to his right to face the basket. Then Embiid stepped back and took an open shot.

During games, Embiid uses the moves he learned at practice.

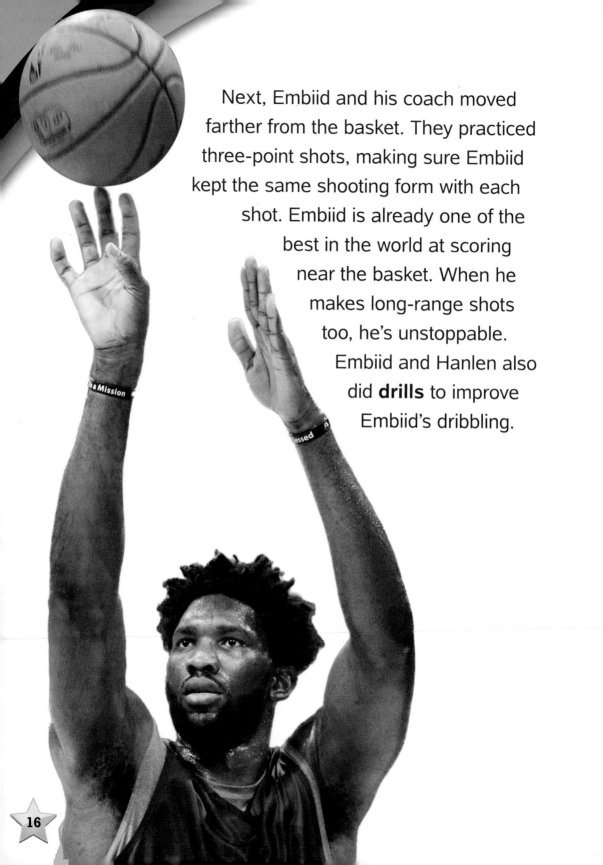

Next, Embiid and his coach moved farther from the basket. They practiced three-point shots, making sure Embiid kept the same shooting form with each shot. Embiid is already one of the best in the world at scoring near the basket. When he makes long-range shots too, he's unstoppable. Embiid and Hanlen also did **drills** to improve Embiid's dribbling.

When Embiid first joined the NBA, he loved junk food and sugary drinks. To improve his diet, he got a personal chef to prepare healthful food. The chef prepares meals specially designed to fuel Embiid's huge body and active lifestyle.

During the season, the 76ers help Embiid stay as fit and healthy as possible. The team provides their superstar with a sleep schedule. They also help him balance his workouts. Workouts in the gym let Embiid build muscle, while workouts on the court improve his skills. The plan has helped make Embiid one of the best and strongest players in the NBA.

Pro athletes get massages to loosen their muscles, which helps prevent injury.

"ANYTHING IS POSSIBLE"

Embiid warms up before a game in 2016.

Embiid launches a shot in the 2019 NBA playoffs.

Thomas Embiid, Joel's father, is an officer in Cameroon's military. He knew that Joel had a future in sports when his tall, athletic son was still a boy. He just didn't think it would be in basketball. Joel's father thought the sport was too rough. He wanted Joel to play pro volleyball in Europe.

Embiid's decision to choose basketball over volleyball has made him a lot of money. In 2017, the 76ers awarded him a five-year contract worth almost $148 million. "I'm so thrilled to be in this position," Embiid posted on Twitter. "I love this city and I'm so, so, so, so excited to be spending my next five years here."

Embiid and other popular players attract attention from celebrities such as Kevin Hart (center).

Socially Active

Embiid loves social media, and his tweets and posts get plenty of attention. He goes to sporting events and writes about the games. He reaches out to celebrities such as Kim Kardashian and Rihanna. He even uses Twitter to try to recruit players such as superstar LeBron James to the 76ers.

Embiid also uses social media to get into the heads of his opponents. He has gotten into online arguments with players such as Willie Reed and Hassan Whiteside. In 2017, Minnesota Timberwolves center Karl-Anthony Towns commented on one of Embiid's social media posts. Towns complained the photo was blurry, and the post was of bad quality. "Better quality than your defense," Embiid responded on Instagram.

Embiid told LeBron James (*right*) that his joining the 76ers would make them champions.

Boys & Girls Clubs provide kids with after-school programs, mentors, and more.

Embiid spends time helping people in the Philadelphia area. He hangs out with kids at Boys & Girls Club events. He shoots baskets and tells the kids about his life in Cameroon and his journey to the NBA. "I just want to show them that anything is possible," he said.

In 2018, Embiid traveled to South Africa with the group Basketball Without Borders. They were on a mission to spread basketball in Africa and give back to communities there. Embiid and his teammates played a special basketball game and hung out with kids. Later, they helped build houses for people in need. Reporters took photos of Embiid as he hauled bricks and painted walls.

Embiid plays basketball with kids in Johannesburg, South Africa.

Though Embiid was drafted in 2014, he didn't play his first professional games until 2016.

One week before the 2014 NBA draft, Embiid's agent shocked the basketball world. He told reporters that Embiid had a broken bone in his foot. The next day, Embiid would have surgery to repair the break.

Embiid's intense playing style means he sometimes crashes into other players.

Some people had thought Embiid would be the top overall pick in the draft. But with the injury, he fell to Philadelphia with the third pick. The team was sure Embiid could be a star, but he missed the entire 2014–2015 season. That season, the 76ers had a terrible 18–64 record.

Even when he wasn't playing, Embiid made sure to practice to keep his skills sharp.

In the summer of 2015, Embiid broke his foot again. Like the first injury, it needed surgery. Embiid missed all of the 2015–2016 season, and some reporters wondered if he'd ever be healthy enough to play. Meanwhile, Philadelphia's 10–72 record was the worst in the NBA.

Embiid finally got healthy, kicking off his rookie season later that year. He played 31 games in 2016–2017 and helped the 76ers' record improve to 28–54. The next season, he played 63 games and led Philadelphia to the playoffs for the first time in six years. They lost to the Boston Celtics.

The team made the playoffs again in 2018–2019, but they fell to the Raptors. Embiid wants to do better in the playoffs, for himself and his team. "Obviously I want to be the best Sixer to ever play here," he said. "To do that, I gotta win championships." Embiid will keep pushing himself to take his team to the top.

Embiid leaps for a dunk in 2019.

All-Star Stats

Due to minor injuries, Embiid missed 18 games in 2018–2019. But when he played, he was a rebounding machine. He averaged 13.6 rebounds per game, second best in the NBA. Where do you think he would have ranked in total rebounds if he had played the entire season?

Most Rebounds in the NBA, 2018–2019

Player	Rebounds
Andre Drummond	1,232
Rudy Gobert	1,041
Nikola Vucevic	960
Karl-Anthony Towns	954
DeAndre Jordan	902
Giannis Antetokounmpo	898
Joel Embiid	871
Nikola Jokic	865
Clint Capela	848
Hassan Whiteside	817

Source Notes

7   "Joel Embiid & Jimmy Butler Postgame Interview
    —Game 6," YouTube video, 11:55, posted by House of
    Highlights, May 9, 2019, https://www.youtube.com
    /watch?v=b3JchErqg90.

11 Jackie MacMullan, "Cameroon Calling," *ESPN the
    Magazine*, May 8, 2017, http://www.espn.com/espn
    /feature/story/_/page/presents19316766/the-key-joel
    -embiid-rise-luc-mbah-moute.

20 Adrian Wojnarowski, "Joel Embiid Agrees to 5-Year,
    $148M Deal with Sixers," *ABC*, October 10, 2017,
    https://6abc.com/sports/joel-embiid-agrees-to-5-year
    -$148m-deal-with-sixers/2513029/.

21 Hector Diaz, "Joel Embiid Gets the Last Laugh after
    Karl-Anthony Towns Tries to Roast Him on Instagram,"
    SBNation, December 14, 2017, https://www.sbnation
    .com/lookit/2017/12/14/16775366/joel-embiid-gets-the
    -last-laugh-after-karl-anthony-towns-tries-to-roast-him
    -on-instagram.

22 Serena Winters, "Ben Simmons, Joel Embiid Give Back
    to Local Communities," *NBC Sports*, October 10, 2018,
    https://www.nbcsports.com/philadelphia/76ers/ben
    -simmons-joel-embiid-give-back-local-communities.

27 Noah Levick, "Joel Embiid Wants to Be the 'Best to Ever
    Do It,' and He Knows What It Will Take to Be Part of the
    Conversation," *NBC Sports Philadelphia*, March 22, 2019,
    https://www.nbcsports.com/philadelphia/76ers/joel
    -embiid-wants-to-be-goat-knows-what-it-will-take-be-part
    -conversation.

Glossary

agent: a person who represents an athlete in business

center: a player who usually stays close to the basket and the middle of the court

conference: a group of teams that play against one another

drills: exercises designed to improve skills

foul: an instance of violating the rules of basketball

free throw: an uncontested shot from behind the free throw line that is sometimes awarded when the other team commits a foul

rebound: the act of grabbing and controlling the ball after a missed shot

recruit: to convince a player to join a team

scholarship: money awarded to a student to help pay for school

scouts: people who judge the skills of athletes

slam dunks: shots made by jumping high into the air and throwing the ball down through the basket

Further Information

Basketball Without Borders
http://global.nba.com/basketball-without-borders/

DeMocker, Michael. *Joel Embiid.* Kennett Square, PA: Purple Toad, 2019.

Jr. NBA
https://jr.nba.com/

Mahoney, Brian. *Basketball's New Wave: The Young Superstars Taking Over the Game.* Burnsville, MN: Press Room Editions, 2019.

Philadelphia 76ers
https://www.nba.com/sixers/

Savage, Jeff. *Basketball Super Stats.* Minneapolis: Lerner Publications, 2018.

Index

Photo Acknowledgments

Image credits: Mitchell Leff/Getty Images, pp. 4, 6, 13, 18, 21, 24, 26; Lance King/Getty Images, p. 8; Maja Hitij - FIFA/FIFA/Getty Images, p. 9; Brian Rothmuller/Icon Sportswire/Getty Images, p. 10; Rich Sugg/Kansas City Star/MCT/Getty Images, pp. 11, 12; CRAIG LASSIG/AFP/Getty Images, p. 14; Vaughn Ridley/Getty Images, pp. 15, 19; Zhong Zhi/Getty Images, p. 16; Mark Brown/Getty Images, p. 17; Kevork S. Djansezian/Getty Images, p. 20; Rich Polk/Getty Images, p. 22; MUJAHID SAFODIEN/AFP/Getty Images, p. 23; Steve Russell/Toronto Star/Getty Images, pp. 25, 27.

Cover image: Jason Miller/Getty Images.